CRAZY CREATURES OF THE ANIMAL KINGDOM

I0811727

WHAT DO YOU KNOW ABOUT ANIMALS WITH POUCHES?

FRANCINE TOPACIO

PowerKiDS press
New York

Published in 2021 by The Rosen Publishing Group, Inc.
29 East 21st Street, New York, NY 10010

Copyright © 2021 by The Rosen Publishing Group, Inc.

All rights reserved. No part of this book may be reproduced in any form without permission in writing from the publisher, except by a reviewer.

First Edition

Portions of this work were originally authored by Marie Racanelli and published as *Animals with Pockets*. All new material in this edition authored by Francine Topacio.

Editor: Kara Murray
Book Design: Tanya Dellaccio

Photo Credits: Cover Rene Becerril/EyeEm/Getty Images; p. 5 Evelyn D. Harrison/Shutterstock.com; pp. 7 (top), 9 CraigRJD/iStock/Getty Images; p. 7 (bottom) D.Bond/Shutterstock.com; p. 11 (both) Edwin Butter/Shutterstock.com; p. 13 Ian Waldie/Getty Images News/Getty Images; p. 15 (top) Susan Flashman/Shutterstock.com; p. 15 (bottom) Frans Lemmens/Corbis Unreleased/Getty Images; p. 17 Mark Newman/The Image Bank/Getty Images; p. 18 Yvonne Van der Horst/Moment/Getty Images; p. 19 Xavier Hoenner Photography/Moment/Getty Images; p. 21 svarshik/iStock/Getty Images; p. 22 Paul Marcellini/Nature Picture Library/Getty Images.

Library of Congress Cataloging-in-Publication Data

Names: Topacio, Francine, author.
Title: What do you know about animals with pouches? / Francine Topacio.
Description: New York : PowerKids Press, [2021] | Series: Crazy creatures of the animal kingdom | Includes index.
Identifiers: LCCN 2019060007 | ISBN 9781725319806 (paperback) | ISBN 9781725319820 (library binding) | ISBN 9781725319813 (6 pack)
Subjects: LCSH: Marsupials—Juvenile literature. | Marsupials—Behavior—Juvenile literature.
Classification: LCC QL737.M3 T67 2021 | DDC 599.2156-dc23
LC record available at https://lccn.loc.gov/2019060007

Manufactured in the United States of America

CPSIA Compliance Information: Batch #CSPK20. For Further Information contact Rosen Publishing, New York, New York at 1-800-237-9932.

Find us on

CONTENTS

MARSUPIALS: THE ANIMALS WITH POCKETS

How many animals can you name? There are so many, and they all come in different sizes, from tiny beings we can't see without special tools to huge elephants and whales. They come in many colors and shapes too. They eat different things as well.

Some of these animals belong to a group called **mammals**. Cats, dogs, lions, and elephants are mammals. People are mammals too! Mammals are warm-blooded animals whose bodies have hair or fur covering most of their skin. They also all feed their babies milk from their bodies. Some of the world's most unusual mammals are **marsupials**. Let's learn more about these animals with pockets!

Marsupial babies, like these opossums, are born and live for a time in their mother's pouch. Once opossum babies come out, they often travel with their mother.

MANY MARSUPIALS

There are more **species** of marsupials than you might think—nearly 300! About 200 of them live in Australia, New Guinea, and the islands near there. Most mammals **native** to that area are marsupials. Australian marsupials can be as small as a mouse or as large as a 6-foot (2 m) tall man. They include kangaroos, wombats, koalas, and more. Some marsupials also live in the Americas.

Marsupials can live in trees or on land. Some like to dig, and others like to climb. One marsupial even lives in water part of the time. Some run or hop very fast, some swim, some glide from trees, and some dig holes in dirt.

Red kangaroos are the world's largest marsupials. When they are born, though, they are tiny. They spend two months growing in the mother's pouch.

HOW STRANGE!

Male red kangaroos are large and powerful! They sometimes fight over females. They will lean back on their strong tails and kick each other with their hind legs.

MARSUPIALS AND THEIR POCKETS

Most marsupials have a pouch of skin where their babies live and grow after they're born. Marsupial babies are very underdeveloped when they are born. They're born early and need special care in order to live. Most of them make their way into their mothers' pouches for this care.

Some marsupials don't have a pouch or have only part of one. They're still marsupials because their babies are born so early in their **development**. The numbat and the antechinus are both marsupials that don't have pockets. Once their babies are born, they find and attach themselves to their mothers and drink milk from her body constantly.

HOW STRANGE!

Numbat mothers are **pregnant** for only 14 days! After the babies are born, they make their way up her body so they can attach and drink her milk for about six months.

The numbat, which is also known as the banded anteater, is a marsupial that lives in Australia. It eats only termites!

TIME IN THE POCKET

When a baby marsupial is born, it's pink and about the size of a jellybean. It can't see, and it's hairless. It's not ready to be on its own yet, not even close! The only parts of newborn marsupials that are well developed are their front legs and sharp claws. The claws help them hang on to their mothers as they climb to the pocket. Their back legs will grow later.

Once they get to the pouch, they attach themselves to their mother and begin to drink milk. The milk helps them grow. Baby marsupials need to stay in the pouch so their bodies can develop.

HOW STRANGE!

Baby marsupials drink their mothers' milk all the time! The mother and baby's bodies work together so that the baby can't let go until it's bigger.

This Bennett's wallaby is just beginning to look around at the outside world! It's been in its mother's pouch for about nine months.

ALL ABOUT MARSUPIALS

1 The kangaroo is likely the best-known marsupial. Kangaroos live in groups called mobs.

2 All baby marsupials are called joeys!

3 Some marsupials have become **extinct**. The desert rat-kangaroo and the thylacine, also called the Tasmanian tiger, are extinct.

4 Most marsupials are **nocturnal**, which means they sleep during the day and hunt and eat at night.

5 Kangaroos and koalas get water from the food they eat. Because of this, they don't need to drink water often, if at all.

6 Marsupials have lots of teeth! Most marsupials have 30 to 50 teeth. Most mammals have 20 to 40 teeth.

7 The pouch looks different in different marsupials. A kangaroo's pouch, which is near the kangaroo's stomach, opens at the top. Mother koalas, opossums, and wombats have pockets that open near their tails or back ends.

8 A wombat's poop is shaped like a cube! When it dries, it becomes very hard and the wombat uses it to mark where it lives and eats.

9 Tasmanian devils are fierce fighters with a powerful bite! They leave no part of the animals they eat behind. They eat the meat, bones, and hair!

TASMANIAN DEVIL

MARSUPIALS IN TREES

Some marsupials, such as the sugar glider and the koala, live in trees. Sugar gliders drink the sap of acacia trees and some eucalyptus trees. They also eat nectar, pollen, and some bugs. They can glide between trees using the thin skin that stretches between their hands and feet. They use their tails to guide them.

Koalas eat only the leaves of eucalyptus trees. However, eucalyptus leaves are hard to **digest** and don't give them much energy. This is why they move slowly and sleep for about 18 hours each day. Koalas have strong claws, two thumbs on each hand, and rough pads on their feet. All these things help them climb trees.

HOW STRANGE!

Koalas have fingerprints that are different for each animal, just like humans do! Scientists think these lines might help them hold on to the trees.

When they're not sleeping, koalas spend their time eating eucalyptus leaves. They each have a home range of several trees that they visit to feed.

WHERE DO MARSUPIALS LIVE?

While some marsupial species spend most of their lives in trees, others live only on land. The Tasmanian devil is a **carnivorous** marsupial native to the Australian island-state of Tasmania. Female Tasmanian devils are usually pregnant for three weeks before they give birth to about four young. The babies are about the size of a raisin. They crawl into the mother's pouch, where they continue to grow for about four months.

The yapok, or water opossum, is the only **aquatic** marsupial species. Yapoks are found in and near bodies of fresh water from Mexico to Argentina. Females give birth to two to five young.

HOW STRANGE!

The yapok is the only species of marsupial in which both males and females have a pouch. However, only females can close the pouch to keep their young dry.

The Tasmanian devil is the world's largest carnivorous marsupial. It can be up to 30 inches (76 cm) long and weigh as much as 26 pounds (12 kg).

THE LIFE OF A WOMBAT

The wombat is another land marsupial. The common wombat and the hairy-nosed wombat are the two main kinds of wombat. These marsupials like to burrow. They are master diggers that use their strong, clawed front feet to dig tunnels, where they sleep. Wombat burrows can be 650 feet (198 m) long. Wombats come out at night to graze on grasses and other plants.

Wombat mothers have one joey every two years. It stays in the mother's pouch for up to 10 months before it starts coming out for short amounts of time. It will continue to drink its mother's milk in the pouch for up to another three months before starting to eat grasses.

Wombats may not look fast. Their strong legs can run as fast as 25 miles (40 km) per hour if they have to, though!

A CLOSER LOOK AT THE KANGAROO

Kangaroos are probably the world's best-known pouched animals. They are known for their big feet and thick tails, which help them balance as they jump. They are plant eaters, and they have special teeth that help them bite off and chew the grasses they eat.

The word "kangaroo" is mostly commonly used for six species, including the eastern grey kangaroo, the western grey kangaroo, and the red kangaroo. The largest is the red kangaroo. It can grow to be about 200 pounds (90 kg) and between 5 and 6 feet (1.5–2 m) tall! The red kangaroo is an amazing jumper. It can cover about 30 feet (9 m) with each jump!

HOW STRANGE!

When the weather gets too hot, kangaroos lick their arms to stay cool. The wetness evaporates, cooling their bodies down.

Newborn kangaroo joeys are about the size of a grape, but they grow fast! At about four months, the joey can hop out for short trips.

THE MARSUPIAL IN YOUR NEIGHBORHOOD

The only native North American marsupial is the Virginia opossum. Don't let its name fool you. This opossum doesn't just live in Virginia but throughout much of the United States. Opossums come out at night to find food. They'll eat nearly anything, including bugs, fruit, and seeds.

No matter where they live, marsupials are interesting animals. Many marsupials, although not the opossum, are **endangered** or close to it because of hunting, predators, and **habitat** destruction. We must learn as much as we can about marsupials so we can keep these strange, wonderful animals safe.

GLOSSARY

aquatic: Living or growing in water.

carnivorous: Eating only meat.

development: The act or process of growing or causing something to grow.

digest: To break down food inside the body so that the body can use it.

endangered: In danger of dying out.

evaporate: To change from water into water vapor.

extinct: No longer existing.

habitat: The natural home for plants, animals, and other living things.

mammal: Any warm-blooded animal whose babies drink milk and whose body is covered with hair or fur.

marsupial: An animal that generally carries its young in a pouch on its body.

native: Living or growing in an area.

nocturnal: Active during the night.

pregnant: Having an unborn baby inside.

species: A group of plants or animals that are all the same kind.

INDEX

WEBSITES

Due to the changing nature of Internet links, PowerKids Press has developed an online list of websites related to the subject of this book. This site is updated regularly. Please use this link to access the list: www.powerkidslinks.com/ccotak/pouches